Bible St...

7 Sessions for Homegroup
and Personal Use

Jeremiah

The passionate prophet

John Houghton

Published 2005 by CWR, Waverley Abbey House, Waverley Lane, Farnham,
Surrey GU9 8EP, England. Registered Charity No. 294387. Registered Limited
Company No. 1990308. Reprinted 2010.

See back of book for list of National Distributors.

Unless otherwise indicated, all Scripture references are from the Holy Bible:
New International Version (NIV), copyright © 1973, 1978, 1984 by the
International Bible Society.

Concept development, editing, design and production by CWR
Cover image: Roger Walker

Printed in Latvia by Yeomans Press Ltd

ISBN: 978-1-85345-372-4

Contents

Introduction

Jeremiah was a prophet of immense passion. His ministry of nearly 50 years encompassed one of the most pivotal periods of world history, the impact of which still affects us today. During that time Jeremiah rose as a prophet of national and international stature whose passionate declarations of the judgment and mercy of God so gripped him as almost to tear him apart.

Jeremiah stood as the voice of truth in the midst of a sea of corruption and deceit. Unafraid to confront religious and political hypocrisy and stupidity, he became the object of persecution and ridicule. Challenging the popular idolatry of his nation and the collapse of morality, he fearlessly declared that sin has dire and inevitable consequences. Judgment would fall, however much people pretended otherwise. With the eye of the true prophet he could already see hostile invasion and ruination on the advancing horizon of history.

It brought Jeremiah no joy to be proved right. Here was a man who loved his people and longed with heartrending intensity that they should return to the good paths of their founding fathers. When Jeremiah preached judgment he did so with tears running down his cheeks, pleading for God's people to heed the warnings and anguished at the consequences that he clearly saw if they refused. In this he identified himself with Jesus who, mourning over the same city centuries later, cried, 'O Jerusalem, Jerusalem, you who kill the prophets and stone those sent to you, how often I have longed to gather your children together, as a hen gathers her chicks under her wings, but you were not willing' (Matt. 23:37).

Jeremiah originated in the family of Hilkiah the priest and came from Anathoth, a town 3 kilometres north of Jerusalem. He was the contemporary of Zephaniah, Habakkuk, Daniel and Ezekiel and exercised his ministry from 627 to about 580 BC. His call heralded a time of minor spiritual revival under the godly king Josiah. Following the rediscovery of the Law of Moses in 622 BC, Josiah instituted a widespread spiritual reform that sought to obliterate idolatry and corruption and restore the true covenant calling of God's people. Sadly, Josiah died in battle against Pharaoh Neco II of Egypt in 609 BC and it marked the end of the nation's hope of renewal. One corrupt king followed another until the eventual fall of Jerusalem in 587 BC at the hands of the Babylonians.

When Jeremiah's ministry began, Assyria and Egypt posed the main threat to Judah, a situation that remained until 605 BC. From then until 586 BC Jeremiah's prophecies focused on the rise of the Babylonian Empire and its implications for his nation. Finally, from 586 to about 580 BC, following the downfall of Judah, he ministered in Jerusalem and Egypt.

Jeremiah dictated his prophecies to Baruch, his secretary, and when king Jehoiakim destroyed the scroll, Jeremiah re-dictated an extended version. All agree that this is his authentic work, as is the book of Lamentations, though the last chapter of Jeremiah is probably penned by Baruch and is largely reproduced in 2 Kings 24:18–25:30.

Most of Jeremiah is a mix of autobiography and sermons addressed to the people of Judah. From chapter 46 onwards, he prophesies against the surrounding nations and declares Babylon's defeat, while the book ends with the record of Jerusalem's fall. The book of Lamentations is a requiem on the whole sorry scene but contains, as always with Jeremiah, the seeds of hope for the future. That future would culminate in the coming of Christ and the turning of captivity into liberation for the whole world. For Jeremiah is a prophet of hope and restoration. God will not forget His promises nor His covenant with the fathers. Sin must be judged so as to purge the race of its idolatry and injustice, but mercy will ultimately triumph over judgment. The redeemed of the Lord will return with joy and gladness.

Jeremiah's potent mix of politics and religion challenges how we look at life. God is the Lord of history and at the national level there is a causal link between morality and judgment, not only for His people but for other nations too. World affairs are not arbitrary, nor are they merely in the hands of men. The hostile invasion by Babylon is a judgment from God, yet Babylon will in time be punished for its sins. God's people will return to their land not because of political enlightenment but because He has purposes that transcend regional power struggles. Jeremiah's message calls us to consider whether we have settled for a God who does not intervene in human affairs and whether we have forgotten that Christ is the Lord of history who rules the nations with an iron rod.

We cannot do justice to the whole of the books of Jeremiah and Lamentations in seven weeks, so the intent of this study is to highlight the key features and to learn the lessons of this great prophet that are applicable to our own day. If judgment must begin at the house of God, then we should wisely heed these words and examine whether we are found wanting. Complacency and compromise are ever-present dangers for the Christian and we continue, in an age that exalts political correctness, social conformity and mere management of the status quo, to need the bracing words of the prophets.

WEEK 1

Inspiration

Opening Icebreaker

Share brief stories of how you first heard the call of God on your lives.

Bible Readings

- Jeremiah 1:1–10
- Psalm 139:13–16
- Isaiah 6:8–9

Key verse: 'Then the LORD reached out his hand and touched my mouth and said to me, "Now, I have put my words in your mouth"' (Jer. 1:9).

Focus: We are all called and inspired to proclaim God's truth.

Opening Our Eyes

The call of Jeremiah is a metaphor for the prophetic calling of the whole Church of Christ and the part we each play in that calling. It reminds us that the proclamation of the truth is at the heart of who we are as God's chosen people (1 Pet. 2:9). This isn't just the responsibility of a few individuals; the call is corporate and it includes all of us who call ourselves Christians.

Jeremiah's call came in his youth. It confronted him with the mystery of God's foreknowledge and the awesome discovery that God had shaped him in his mother's womb for this time and purpose. This would provide a fundamental relational security for a man who must live through difficult times. Psalm 139:13–16 teaches us that we are more than pre-programmed DNA and ancestral genes. Each of us is individually known and shaped by a loving heavenly Father from the time of our conception. As with Jeremiah, we may come to realise that there is a will of God for our lives that is bound up with greater purposes than we can ever imagine (Rom. 8:29–30).

Not that this stopped Jeremiah from protesting! As with ourselves he felt inadequate, inexperienced and unskilled for the role he would play. Yet this sensitive, emotional and self-effacing man is chosen by God to take spiritual authority over national destinies. His ministry will be both destructive and constructive – pulling down and destroying the strongholds of evil and then building and planting righteousness.

It serves to remind us that we are not called to be blandly nice. Much as we do not wish to cause offence by our attitudes or conduct, we are people who belong to a different kingdom with different values. We are called to challenge the world's abuse of God's will. We must speak up for the sufferings of the poor and the victims of moral and spiritual corruption. We proclaim the reality of human sinfulness and the need to repent. We declare salvation through the sacrificial blood of Christ. This gospel is a stumbling stone to the religious and madness to the secular humanist (1 Cor. 1:22–25). Yet proclaim it we must.

Disobedience proved to be scarcely an option for Jeremiah. God promised to protect him and to give him the words to say. What more could he ask for? Isaiah had a similar experience (Isa. 6:8–9).

The times were significant. History was about to change and Jeremiah is given two visions:

The first is of an almond branch with God saying He is watching to see that His Word is fulfilled. This is a wordplay on the Hebrew for almond. In English, we might say, 'I see a pear branch' and God is peering to see that His Word is fulfilled.

The second vision is of a boiling cauldron from the north. There is judgment coming because of the breach of covenant, the idolatry and corruption that characterised the nation. It will be delivered at the hands of the emergent Babylonian Empire. Bringing such words will provoke opposition and Jeremiah's voice will be lonely; religious professionals and politicians alike will proclaim the opposite (Jer. 14:13–16). There will be times when Jeremiah will wish he had never been born (Jer. 20:14–18). He will not marry (Jer. 16:1) for there will be no cause for celebration in his lifetime. Yet, sombre as this seems, the good fruits of Jeremiah's ministry continue to this day.

Discussion Starters

1. The meaning of life is to know and to do the will of God. In what ways have you found this to be true?

_____

_____

_____

_____

_____

2. Share occasions when you have felt very directly that God has given you words to speak.

_____

_____

_____

_____

_____

3. If the Church is the *ekklesia*, 'the called out ones', what is it called out for?

_____

_____

_____

_____

_____

4. Why do we sometimes find ourselves ashamed of Jesus?

_____

_____

_____

_____

_____

5. If you were a prophet to our nation, what do you feel are the issues that you would address?

_____

_____

_____

_____

_____

6. Most prophecy in the Bible is in the form of poetry and often includes vivid imagery. Have you experienced a prophetic dream? What was the nature of it?

_____

_____

_____

_____

_____

7. Joel prophesied that we would be a prophetic people when the Spirit came. To what extent do you think we are?

_____

_____

_____

_____

_____

Personal Application

The true Church of Christ will continue to raise its voice
globally against injustice and idolatry. It must do so
under the inspiration of the Holy Spirit and proclaim
both judgment upon sin and mercy to the penitent (John
16:8–10). The Word of God is still a two-edged sword
and we must use both blades equally. In our own lives
we need the bracing sense of God's call to proclaim His
truth faithfully in our generation. It will take courage and
conviction, coupled with compassion, for judgment is
most surely coming on the earth. It may be at the hands
of nations, but will certainly be the case when our risen
Jesus returns in glory (Acts 17:30–31). Are you willing to
respond to the call of God upon your life?

Seeing Jesus in the Scriptures

Jesus was a fiery prophet who was likened to Elijah
(though that comparison properly belonged to John the
Baptist). He was not afraid to denounce hypocrisy and
corruption. In human terms, such provocation led to
His death. Yet through this paradox God was in Christ
reconciling the world to Himself. The Word made flesh
brought both judgment and hope, death and resurrection.
Losing our lives so that we might find life is the heart
of His message. As we acknowledge the prophetic
truth about ourselves, however humbling that is, so we
receive the truth about Him and discover the wonder of
redemption. For in spite of the necessarily strong words,
Jesus did not come with the intent of condemning us but
of saving us.

WEEK 2

Proclamation

Opening Icebreaker

List ten truths your non-Christian neighbours need to know.

Bible Readings

- Jeremiah 2:1–8
- Romans 1:18–23
- Galatians 6:1–16

Key verse: 'Has a nation ever changed its gods? (Yet they are not gods at all.) But my people have exchanged their Glory for worthless idols' (Jer. 2:11).

Focus: Idolatry destroys nations and individuals alike.

Opening Our Eyes

Jeremiah brought nine major prophecies over the long years of his ministry. These were addressed to the remaining southern kingdom of Judah – the northern kingdom, Israel, having gone into captivity years earlier. At the heart of his ministry lay the Sinaitic covenant into which God's people had freely entered and which provided their national identity.

Jeremiah opens his ministry by proclaiming that the pure young bride covenanted to Yahweh has become a prostitute. Carnal in heart and shameless in behaviour, she has embraced worthless idols and in doing so has made herself worthless. How astonishing that a nation should change its gods: no longer worshipping the Creator, Judah now has as many gods as towns. But these false gods of fertility, child sacrifice and occult knowledge are in reality rubbish.

Judah's idolatry has political consequences. In forsaking the spring of living water and digging leaky cisterns, they have entrusted themselves to the polluted political waters of the Nile (Egypt) and the Euphrates (Assyria). These will fail.

The Lord says that he has tried to correct Judah from her waywardness, but she refused to respond. Nor was she prepared to learn from Israel's folly. Her northern sister had permitted the same sins and had fallen under judgment. Israel had been invaded by Assyria in 721 BC and the capital, Samaria, had fallen. This leaves Judah even more culpable. For the full force of this spiritual adultery see Ezekiel 16 and 23.

Although Jeremiah acknowledges the possibility of Judah, and even Israel, repenting and finding mercy, it won't happen. So hard is Judah's heart that she has gone down the road of no return. Judgment is at the gates, but even as the enemy advances, Judah tarts herself up in the vain hope of seducing her foe. Jeremiah searches the streets in vain to find a person of integrity. He searches among the leaders, but rulers, priests and prophets alike, they all tell lies. They say, 'Peace, peace,' when there is no peace.

Idolatry, and the demise of true faith in God to a mere folk memory, leads inevitably to social injustice. Jeremiah cries out against the exploitation of the vulnerable. There is one law for the rich and another for the poor. Children are offered in sacrifice to Molech in the valley of Hinnom – an act so terrible that it was beyond the divine comprehension. Deceit ruled relationships and business alike. These people were nominally the chosen race, the circumcised, but their hearts were uncircumcised. It is a familiar theme and taken up by the apostle Paul in Galatians 6:12–16.

Jeremiah returns constantly to the root cause of injustice; it is the stupidity of trusting in idols. They are like scarecrows – they have no power to harm and they do no good. Idols are made by men from natural materials and like them they will perish. By contrast, Jeremiah reminds his hearers that God made the universe. Even when a drought fell upon Judah, the people did not turn back to their Creator-Redeemer, but continued worshipping idols that could bring no rain.

When we consider our own nation, we find many parallels between Jeremiah's world and our own – Romans 1:18–23. If we lose a belief in a Creator, if we forsake the Ten Commandments which are the divine basis for social justice, then corruption, abuse, decadence and collapse will inevitably follow. Only faith in God's Son, Jesus Christ our Redeemer, can restore such a fallen humanity. It is a sober message, but one that we dare not shirk from if we value the future.

Discussion Starters

1. Judah was a theocracy, unlike our own nation. To what extent can we apply Jeremiah's charges and warnings to our nation? Or do they apply only to the Church?

_____

_____

_____

_____

2. How do you think spiritual adultery manifests itself today?

_____

_____

_____

_____

3. Discuss the relationship between sin and disaster. Is there any connection?

_____

_____

_____

_____

4. People didn't listen to Jeremiah but he spoke the truth anyway. On what issues do you think we need to speak out even if it makes us unpopular?

_____

_____

_____

_____

5. Jeremiah warns us not to exploit the vulnerable. Who are the vulnerable in our society, and what can we do to help them?

_____

_____

_____

_____

6. How do you uncover false peace in people's lives?

_____

_____

_____

_____

7. What is circumcision of the heart?

_____

_____

_____

_____

8. If idols are fraudulent, how does that affect our stance on other religions?

_____

_____

_____

_____

Personal Application

What is true of nations is true of individuals. We live in an age of religious pluralism and syncretism (all religions contain the truth and we can pick-and-mix as we please) which substitutes for the truth of a Creator God in whom we live and move and have our being (Acts 17:28). Beliefs produce behaviour. We need to renounce idolatry whether it is in the mind or on the mantelpiece (1 John 5:21). Only then will we discover the good and perfect will of God for our lives and for our society. Let us not compromise our faith in Christ for the idolatry that sneaks in under the name of tolerance and political correctness.

Seeing Jesus in the Scriptures

Jesus declared, 'I am the way and the truth and the life. No-one comes to the Father except through me' (John 14:6). He is the only Saviour of mankind, the only true light, the only living water, the only good shepherd who laid down His life for the sheep. Jesus is the eternal Word made flesh, the true image of God. However much we may respect the religious beliefs of others, we must recognise idolatry for what it is. Idols will not save souls, nor transform nations. 'Salvation is found in no-one else, for there is no other name under heaven given to men by which we must be saved' (Acts 4:12).

WEEK 3

Supplication

Opening Icebreaker

What is the most passionate prayer you have ever prayed?

Bible Readings

- Jeremiah 14:7–22
- 2 Chronicles 7:13–15
- 1 Timothy 2:1–4

Key verse: 'O Lord, we acknowledge our wickedness and the guilt of our fathers; we have indeed sinned against you' (Jer. 14:20).

Focus: We must pray for our nation, identifying ourselves with its sinfulness, and seeking God's mercy.

Opening Our Eyes

Effective intercession springs from an underlying passion that, however timidly or fervently it is expressed, longs for God to intervene in the world. Such a powerful act is not for the lazy, the indifferent or the casual. To pray is to endeavour to change the course of history.

Jeremiah's passion was born from a deep love for God and for his wayward people. He was truly heartbroken over their folly and was able with the eyes of a prophet to see that they were on course for disaster (Jer. 9:1–2). No one should preach judgment without tears in their eyes and prayers for mercy in their heart.

The occasion of Jeremiah's supplication was a series of disastrous droughts that he understood to be the first warnings of the impending political disaster. Harvests were failing and the animals dying, yet still the people believed that it was because they had not made enough offerings to their idols.

Jeremiah acknowledges the sins of the people and identifies himself with those sins. He calls upon God, the hope of Israel, to have mercy for His name's sake. It is an appeal to the graciousness of God's character, a recognition that the Lord prefers mercy to judgment and does not willingly punish.

Prayer is a dialogue and not always a comfortable one. Jeremiah is told not to pray for the people's good because it is too late and judgment is coming – sword, famine and pestilence! Jeremiah protests that the professional prophets say otherwise, there will be peace in our time. 'Not so,' says the Lord. This does not stop Jeremiah from protesting and seeking to change the mind of the Lord. He, if no one else, acknowledges the wickedness of the nation and he pleads with God to honour His covenant.

He knows that the idols cannot bring rain and so, representing the faithful remnant, puts his faith in God.

Jeremiah is told to bury a linen belt and later to dig it up, only to find it was mildewed, good for nothing. So God will ruin the pride of Judah. The prophet can see a great funeral coming and he calls for the wailing women to mourn. He cries to God that His fury should be poured out on the ungodly who have persecuted His people, but it is too late.

Why pray when it is obvious that your prayers will not be answered? Surely those who pray as Jeremiah did demonstrate that at least their hearts are right with God. They are also a signpost to the future. Intercessors are people who live out of their time and who, by their prayers and the uprightness of their hearts, keep the faith without which there will be no future. Demonstrating a true heart is more important than whether or not our prayers are answered.

The reason Jeremiah's prayers could not be answered lay not with God or with Jeremiah, but with the refusal of the people to repent. Prayer alone does not produce repentance; conviction of sin is a response to the Word of God that Jeremiah had proclaimed faithfully. So, however much God and Jeremiah desired judgment to be averted, the wilful people brought this on themselves. Prayer and proclamation must go hand in hand. We cannot repent for others; they must do that for themselves. What we can do is to identify with the sins of the fathers in so far as we are party to those same sins and we maintain injustices that were caused by their unrighteousness. It is at least a starting point.

Discussion Starters

1. What was revealed in Jeremiah's prayers that made his preaching so effective?

   _____

   _____

   _____

   _____

2. Discuss your motives for praying for the nation. Is it for your sake or for God's?

   _____

   _____

   _____

   _____

3. What sort of prayer of contrition would you write for our nation?

   _____

   _____

   _____

   _____

4. Jeremiah felt so grieved that he questioned God's goodness (Jer. 15:18–19). When are we tempted to do that?

   _____

   _____

   _____

   _____

5. Organise a group prayer walk around your neighbourhood.

_____

_____

_____

_____

6. Discuss biblical examples of when a prayer has turned away judgment.

_____

_____

_____

_____

7. Do you think we are facing a time of God's judgment or God's mercy? How will you respond to your answer?

_____

_____

_____

_____

8. In what ways can your group pray more effectively for the nation?

_____

_____

_____

_____

Personal Application

It is very easy to criticise and find fault with both the Church and our nation. Our news media do this on a daily basis and we, in Britain, have a reputation for being a nation of cynical gripers and moaners. But merely criticising or bemoaning the state of affairs will change nothing. We need to pray, and earnestly so. Our prayers must be for the mercy of God to fall upon a sinful nation. Paul instructs Timothy to make it a priority to pray for all people and all authorities so that our lives might be peaceful and devout and that the climate should be conducive to the gospel (1 Tim. 2:1–4). Do we take this seriously?

Seeing Jesus in the Scriptures

Jesus was a man of great passion. During His days on earth He offered earnest prayer to God. His prayers in Gethsemane are well known, but this was clearly characteristic of His whole life (Heb. 5:7). He was known to rise early for prayer, and sometimes to spend whole nights in prayer. The disciples were so impressed with Jesus' prayer life that they asked Him to teach them how to pray (Luke 11:1). Jesus continues to pray for us since He is our great High Priest who '… is able to save completely those who come to God through him, because he lives always to intercede for them' (Heb. 7:25). When we intercede for others we do so as members of Christ's royal priesthood.

WEEK 4

Confrontation

Opening Icebreaker

Give examples of when you have had to confront
people with the error of their ways for their own good.
Did it work?

Bible Readings

- Jeremiah 26:8–13
- Proverbs 31:8–9
- Ezekiel 3:16–20
- Acts 4:18–31

Key verse: 'Now reform your ways and your actions and
obey the LORD your God. Then the LORD will relent and
will not bring the disaster he has pronounced against you'
(Jer. 26:13).

Focus: We have a responsibility to confront evil, to warn
of its consequences, and to call for reform.

Opening Our Eyes

Jeremiah was a prophet to the nations and in particular to his own. The role involved him in political controversy. The nation was in a bad state and the leaders were using sticking plaster to treat a serious and life-threatening ailment. The covenant that had bound the nation together under God was broken. Judah had torn up the constitution and the social and political consequences were dire. Leaders and people had to make a choice between returning to the good path of Moses or of continuing in idolatrous rebellion.

Confrontation led to persecution and to a plot against Jeremiah's life by the men of his own town. He does not find his role an easy one and at times indulges in a pity party (Jer. 15:15–18). For here is a man who takes no pleasure in spouting controversial opinions, but is nonetheless profoundly compelled by the Word of God to tell the truth.

The political leaders encouraged idolatry and supported injustice, so they were a target for Jeremiah's words. He took an earthenware flask and broke it to demonstrate how God would break Judah because of its child abuse and child sacrifice. The act aroused the anger of Pashhur who had Jeremiah beaten up and put in stocks. It led to Jeremiah changing Pashhur's name to Magor-Missabib, which means 'terror on every side'. Jeremiah also confronted King Jehoiakim who was ripping off the people for his own gain. This led to the king burning Jeremiah's prophecies, an act that was considered sacrilegious even by the standards of the decadent court officials. Jeremiah simply re-dictated his prophecies to his faithful secretary, Baruch. At one point the prophet faced the death penalty for treason and was only saved by the intervention of some God-fearing officials.

In spite of persecution and dislike by the kings and officials, Jeremiah was a voice to be reckoned with and, during Zedekiah's reign, the king consulted him and asked him to prophesy deliverance from Nebuchadnezzar. Needless to say, Jeremiah did the opposite and advocated surrender to the Babylonians as the best policy. Later on he made a wooden yoke and said, 'Serve Nebuchadnezzar or die'. He advised Zedekiah not to listen to fools who imagine they can withstand the might of Babylon. One such fool was the false prophet Hananiah, who in a theatrical gesture broke Jeremiah's yoke. Jeremiah simply replaced the wooden one with an iron one to make the point. Zedekiah imagined that Egypt would relieve Jerusalem, but that would not happen. Jeremiah was falsely charged with desertion and was put in prison. Later on he was dropped into a muddy cistern to die. The king retained some vestige of respect for the prophet and put him under house arrest – an event that doubtless saved Jeremiah's life.

One of Jeremiah's painful and lonely tasks was to confront the false prophets of Baal, who were adulterous liars conjuring up false visions from their own minds. Their dreams of safety and security simply assured a decent pay cheque, whereas Jeremiah was made of sterner stuff and in spite of his personal discomfort told the truth. There has to be a point in life when we determine to follow the Lord and to speak the Word of God with boldness. In the long run truth will be vindicated even if it is despised at the time of its delivery. Jeremiah's words proved to be absolutely right and it was his enemies who were ultimately confounded.

Discussion Starters

1. How do you confront false religion in a pluralistic society?

2. Jeremiah's prophecies were directed politically. How should we engage politically today?

3. Jesus is a rock of stumbling to unbelievers. What does this mean?

4. How can the Church positively confront sin?

5. How far are we prepared to go to tell the truth?

_____

_____

_____

_____

_____

6. What is the intent of confronting people with their sin? How do you help them?

_____

_____

_____

_____

_____

7. Identify the sins that the Church needs to repent of, including those we are party to ourselves.

_____

_____

_____

_____

_____

Personal Application

It takes courage to confront evil. Nobody much likes a whistle-blower. Sometimes bringing the truth of God's Word will challenge vested interests and personal reputations. Yet, if we are to be faithful to God, we must tell it like it is. Jeremiah spoke up on behalf of the exploited poor, the sacrificed children and the victims of injustice. We must do the same wherever we can have influence. A Christianity that does not express itself in love for our neighbour is a false spirituality (1 John 4:20–21). Such love must be practical (1 John 3:17–18). We must ask ourselves where we need to speak and to act (Prov. 31:8–9) and then get on and do it.

Seeing Jesus in the Scriptures

Jesus confronted the hypocrisy and vested self-interest of the Pharisees with ruthless effectiveness. He did so because He saw how this prevented people from experiencing the true knowledge of God and sustained a political regime that ultimately would perish. It did so in AD 70 with the fall of Jerusalem. He calls us to be the salt of the earth, which means we are there to oppose corruption in all its forms.

His Nazareth manifesto proclaimed good news to the poor and liberty to the oppressed. It carried by implication a challenge, calling the oppressors to repent of their iniquity. So the Church today must use its spiritual weapons to bring the justice of Jesus to an unequal world that is more often than not managed by self-seeking politicians and multinational businesses.

WEEK 5

Devastation

Opening Icebreaker

Everyone agrees the world will end sometime. List up to ten popular 'how the world will end' scenarios. Which is most likely?

Bible Readings

- Jeremiah 25:1–13
- 2 Kings 21:1–9
- Hebrews 12:26–28
- Revelation 19:1–8

Key verse: "'But you did not listen to me,' declares the LORD, "and you have provoked me with what your hands have made, and you have brought harm to yourselves'" (Jer. 25:7).

Focus: Persistent sin carries inevitable consequences and these may swallow up the righteous along with the wicked.

Opening Our Eyes

Jeremiah's political judgment being inspired by God proved to be spot on, though he wished passionately that he was wrong. Time and again in the public forums he had acted out in vivid poetry the scenario of invasion, siege and collapse. God would send His destroyers – sword, wild dogs, birds of prey and predatory beasts – because the nation persisted in the unjust, idolatrous and wicked sins of Manasseh (2 Kings 21:1–9).

Jeremiah had prophesied unheeded for some 23 years. The judgment was long coming, not because he was mistaken, but because God is slow to anger and always gives us opportunity to repent (Exod. 34:5–7). But when it did finally come it was devastating. Nebuchadnezzar invaded Judah and put Jerusalem under a ruinous siege. In all, there were three deportations of the people to Babylon. The first in 605 BC, the second in 597 BC and the third in 587 BC. Babylonian policy was to invite surrender with minimum blood loss, but where that failed then to act ruthlessly. The arrogance and self-deception of Judah's rulers brought about by their idolatry, induced them to put up a futile resistance to Babylon. As Jeremiah had warned, it was a fatal mistake. His patience exhausted, and God's final offer of mercy rejected by Jerusalem's leaders, in 587 BC Nebuchadnezzar, king of Babylon, destroyed the walls of Jerusalem and razed the Temple to the ground.

It is hard to gauge the horror of that time. People ate their own children in desperation to survive starvation. Inflation went through the roof as the famine took life after life. And when the walls finally fell the Babylonian sword slaughtered without mercy. Of the survivors, those of status or skill, in all some 4,600 key people, were deported to Babylon leaving the land bereft of leadership, culture and trade. The Judah of David and Solomon, the world centre of monotheism, was ruined beyond measure and reduced to the status of a rural vassal to a pagan empire. The chaos was unimaginable. The Temple was destroyed and its goods taken to Babylon as plunder. The army had fled in disarray and to all intents and purposes the nation was finished.

For the people the unthinkable had happened. God had not protected them. Jeremiah had been proved right. Indeed so much so that Nebuchadnezzar had spared him and this great prophet was perhaps the only truly free man left in Jerusalem. Many of those who remained wanted to flee to Egypt in the hope of finding sanctuary and support from that nation. Jeremiah warned that this would be folly upon folly; they would be better off under Nebuchadnezzar. Nonetheless, they insisted on going and compelled Jeremiah to accompany them to Taphanes. Jeremiah, as acutely open to the voice of God as ever, prophesied that Egypt would fall, as also would the surrounding nations of the Philistines, Moab, Ammon, Edom, Damascus, Kedar, Hazor and Elam.

To gauge the extent of Judah's blindness, the refugees, especially the women, continued to worship the Queen of Heaven (Jer. 7.18) in the incredulous belief that she had given them plenty and it was the failure to worship her that had led to the fall of Jerusalem. Not only was the centre of faith destroyed, it appeared that the faith itself had died.

Yet, in the purposes of God the seed of the future was already planted. Jeremiah prophesied that the land would be desolate for 70 years – no less, but no more.

Discussion Starters

1. How would you address a not-yet-believer on current conflicts and catastrophes in the light of Jesus' words in Matthew 25:6–8?

_____

_____

_____

_____

2. War confronts us with the sober realities of judgment. How do you think we can help to preserve peace in the world?

_____

_____

_____

_____

3. Disasters seem indiscriminate. How do you align this with the love of God?

_____

_____

_____

_____

4. Hebrews 12:26–28 speaks of a great shaking of the nations and of an emerging unshakeable kingdom. What does this mean?

_____

_____

_____

_____

5. What comfort would you offer to someone who has undergone a personal devastation such as the loss of loved ones in a car accident?

_____

_____

_____

_____

6. What would be your survival strategy if you lost everything?

_____

_____

_____

_____

7. Is war the judgment of God, the work of the devil, or the consequence of man's falling? How do you differentiate?

_____

_____

_____

_____

Personal Application

God normally speaks quietly, but He speaks loudly in times of crisis. Sudden devastation can affect nations, communities, families and individuals. The reasons for this are often complex and may appear random, especially in the short term. We may be the victims of other people's follies as well as our own. Times of trouble should be times of reflection and times when we cling to our only true Rock. It may be tempting to feel that God has failed us and that other world-views have more to offer, but this is when the reality of our faith will be proved. Jeremiah kept the faith, as did the others who never surrendered to idolatry. Let us do the same.

Seeing Jesus in the Scriptures

Jesus foresaw the fall of Jerusalem. It would take place in AD 70 at the hands of the Romans when once again the city had rebelled against an empire and had trusted in its own security (Matt. 24:1–2). He used the disciples' question to fast forward history and incorporate both the fall of Jerusalem, the traumatic events at the end of the age, and His personal return in power and great glory (Matt. 24:30). Then would come the final judgment of the nations and the creation of a new heaven and a new earth in which righteousness dwelt. In the light of these forthcoming events, Jesus calls us to be prepared for His return by serving Him faithfully.

WEEK 6

Lamentation

Opening Icebreaker

What is the saddest story you have ever heard?

Bible Readings

- Lamentations 1:1–12
- Psalm 137:1–9
- Isaiah 53:1–3

Key verse: 'Is it nothing to you, all you who pass by? Look around and see. Is any suffering like my suffering that was inflicted on me, that the LORD brought on me in the day of his fierce anger?' (Lam. 1:12).

Focus: Lamenting is the proper expression of grief that gives birth to the future.

Opening Our Eyes

The violent destruction and death of a city is a terrible thing. It was left to Jeremiah to write the funeral elegy for Jerusalem. He was witnessing the death of a culture and the destruction of a faith. God's covenant to give the land to Abraham and his descendants for ever lay smouldering in the ashes. Judah has committed spiritual adultery and not considered her future. Now her deeds had caught up with her. She was a deserted and ruined woman to whom no comfort could be brought.

Jeremiah acknowledges the sins and gives poetic voice to the necessary words of repentance. He does not blame God for His ruthless judgment, because it was fully justified. Behind every attribution of blame against God for grievous circumstances, lies a heart of pride that refuses to acknowledge either personal or national guilt or the fallenness of human nature. Judah had been led astray by false prophets, men pleasers who denied the truth in exchange for personal gain. As a consequence the Word of God had dried up in the land and the people were bereft of hope. So manifest was the folly of the nation that her enemies now mocked her, forcing her eyes to look upon the ruins of the city. 'Is this Zion the perfection of beauty?' they taunted. 'Sing us one of the songs of Zion!' But by the rivers of Babylon there was no heart for music (Psa. 137:1–4).

Jeremiah had witnessed the terrible horror of famine, cannibalism and death. Everything had a price on it in the futile struggle for survival. The prophet expresses the wish that he could have lived at a different time. He is an old man trapped by history and as he surveys the scene and weeps, he sees that the noble classes are as ruined as everyone else. Priest and elders are all unclean. Princes have become paupers and die like the rest.

There was little to encourage hope in the midst of this
tragedy. Yet, even in this poem of mourning, Jeremiah's
faith rises. God's compassion does not fail. Mercy is
renewed every morning and great is His faithfulness (Lam.
3:22–27). It is well to remind ourselves, during times
of disaster, that God does not willingly judge. He takes
no delight in the death of the wicked (2 Pet. 3:9). So,
Jeremiah, although filled with despair, can still appeal to
God for mercy and for a better future.

Grieving appears to be a lost art in the West. Requiems
are rare. Lamenting is scorned. Yet, it is a cleansing
process and an important part of human experience.
Much of the book of Psalms seeks to give voice to
grief and anguish. How sad then that most Christian
songwriters ignore those parts, leaving us with a clap-
happy facile optimism detached from the truth of the
human condition. Afraid of deeper feelings we substitute
analysis for sorrow and glib platitudes for heart-rending
anguish. Christians may not grieve without hope, but
that doesn't mean they shouldn't grieve at all and there
is cause enough for lament in our modern world. When
we consider whether at home or abroad the tragedies of
life, more might be learned in grief than in comedy. The
grave when properly acknowledged and lamented can
become the seedbed of new life. In the words of George
Matheson, 'I lay in dust life's glory dead, and from the
ground there blossoms red, life that shall endless be.'

Discussion Starters

1. There is a time to mourn. Why do you think we hide from grief and mourning?

2. To explore the importance of facing grief, you could listen to a requiem mass.

3. Failure to lament is a cause of much psychological illness. Discuss this.

4. Given all the suffering in the world, why do you think many churches never sing the darker parts of the Psalms?

Lamentation

5. Grief is the price we pay for love. Discuss.

_____
_____
_____
_____
_____

6. How can we remember the devastated Church in different parts of the world where persecution is intense?

_____
_____
_____
_____
_____

7. We do not grieve without hope. How would you share that hope with a not-yet-believer?

_____
_____
_____
_____
_____

Personal Application

Christians should not be afraid to grieve, nor feel that by doing so they are betraying the faith and letting down the side. Death is still the last enemy to be destroyed and while it stalks the earth, it is proper to lament the ravages of its pathway. When we consider the moral ruination of society, the consequences of wars, famines and commercial exploitation, the enslavement of children, soaring abortion figures and the environmental disasters, then surely we should grieve and give voice to that in lament. Only then will we be cleansed, instructed and inspired to make the world a better place.

Seeing Jesus in the Scriptures

'Jesus wept.' It is the shortest verse in the Bible, but one that confronts us with the true humanity of the Son of God. This is not a theological statement. He wept because His friend was dead and because He shared the sorrow of Lazarus' grieving family, even though He anticipated that a miracle might take place at the tomb.

Our Lord is described as a man of sorrows and acquainted with grief and we find Him grieving over the ills of the human race, sorrowing over Jerusalem. Although Jesus faced His own death with immense courage and determination in the Garden of Gethsemane He grieved for the impending loss of His own young life. Let us be grateful that we do not have a High Priest who is detached from our humanity, but one able to sympathise because He has been tempted in every way, just as we are.

WEEK 7

Restoration

Opening Icebreaker

Share examples of when you have been involved in a restoration. This may have been something like restoring a derelict garden or an old car, or it may be the restoration of a personal relationship.

Bible Readings

- Jeremiah 23:5–6
- Jeremiah 29:11–14
- Psalm 126:1–6
- Hebrews 8:1–13

Key verse: "'For I know the plans I have for you,' declares the LORD, "plans to prosper you and not to harm you, plans to give you hope and a future'" (Jer. 29:11).

Focus: Behind God's judgment lay His mercy and His plan to inaugurate a new covenant in Christ.

Opening Our Eyes

Hints that God's anger would not last forever appear like poppies on a battlefield throughout Jeremiah's prophecies. So, in Jeremiah 12:15–16 God promises to return and have compassion on His people and restore them to their land. God has a future purpose for His people and, in a startling projection into the far future, promises that in place of the false shepherds, who had scattered the sheep, God will raise up a Branch of Righteousness – a King who will bring justice to the world and be known as 'The LORD Our Righteousness' (Jer. 23:5–6). The New Testament, especially the book of Hebrews, recognises Jesus as the fulfilment of this prophecy. The promised Messiah will inaugurate a new covenant for a new day. It will supersede and be unlike the old covenant which God's people had broken. Under this new covenant the Law would be written not on tablets of stone, but on the hearts of the people. God will not be distant, but known personally by all, and the sins and iniquities of God's people will be for ever forgotten (Jer. 31:31–34). The book of Hebrews makes clear that this is fulfilled in the gospel message concerning Jesus (Heb. 8:1–13).

Before this can happen, God's people must be restored to their land and the faith purified and revitalised. Jeremiah had a vision of two baskets of figs (Jer. 24:1–10). Those who remained in the corrupted land would be bad figs, whereas the good figs, although feeling the opposite, would go into exile and later return. The necessary change of heart would occur not in Jerusalem, but in Babylon. After 70 years in captivity, God's people, for ever purified from the follies of fertility cult worship, would be restored. So, he writes a letter encouraging the captive exiles to settle down in Babylon and seek the city's good. The Lord has good plans for them, to give them a future and a hope (Jer. 29:11–14). As they search for God with their whole heart the Lord will graciously respond in reconciliation. Ignore the false prophets who say otherwise. They will be destroyed.

This restoration is so certain that Jeremiah is instructed to invest in a field even while he is under house arrest, and the fall of Jerusalem grows ever more imminent. It is a prophetic act to say that God's people will once more invest their lives back in the land.

This might seem impossible at the present, but the faith and the people will not be lost. Indeed, indestructible Babylon will be destroyed. Although God has disciplined His people with great severity it is not for their annihilation but for their restoration. Humbled by their guilt and sick with remorse they will be healed. Jerusalem itself will be rebuilt and the sadness of the Babylonian riverside will be replaced by astonished laughter and singing (Psa. 126:1–3).

Harvests will abound. For God is ultimately their Father, not their enemy (Jer. 31:9). The timing of this will be after 70 years. This was no arbitrary figure. The Sabbath had been abused for so long, that a debt to the land had to be paid (2 Chron. 36:21). The exiled prophet Daniel understood this and in the first year of Darius, prayed a prayer of repentance that turned the key in the lock of history. It led to the political and spiritual restoration of God's people to their land, the rebuilding of the Temple, and ultimately the coming of Jesus, the Messiah.

Discussion Starters

1. The fundamental principle of the universe is that life is born out of death (John 12:24). Share your understanding and experience of this truth.

_____

_____

_____

_____

2. Why did God decree 70 years captivity for His people? See Jeremiah 25:8–13 and Daniel 9:1–4ff.

_____

_____

_____

_____

3. How would you tell the story of the Prodigal Son to a backslidden believer?

_____

_____

_____

_____

4. Identify the good things that God brought out of the Babylonian captivity.

_____

_____

_____

_____

5. What does the return of God's people teach us about the character of God?

_____

_____

_____

_____

6. Discuss the new covenant implications of Jeremiah 33. 31v33 ??

_____

_____

_____

_____

7. What does it mean to you when the psalmist says, '... he restores my soul' (Psa. 23:3)?

_____

_____

_____

_____

Personal Application

The Christian life is an ascending spiral of death and resurrection experiences, energised by the Holy Spirit. We will experience purifying times of grief and inspiring times of restoration. It happens in church life as well as in our personal experience. We should celebrate the times of refreshing that the Lord grants. They are precious seasons for growth and adventure, for expansion and attainment. We should receive such blessings with thanksgiving and celebration, and in anticipation of that coming day when death will cease and life will be truly everlasting. We live already in the day of grace, the time of Jubilee when Jesus is setting His people free to experience the glorious liberty of the sons of God. Let the blessing flow from your lives to all those who need liberating from spiritual captivity.

Seeing Jesus in the Scriptures

The Messianic line promised as far back as Genesis 3 was challenged, threatened and almost destroyed by a combination of satanic seduction, imperial aggression and human sinfulness. Yet God remained faithful to His covenant and committed to His promise that the Seed of the woman would come to bring salvation to the world. Even the birth of Christ was harassed, as Jeremiah prophesied (Jer. 31:15) and Matthew recorded (Matt. 2:16–18). Jesus' coming would herald a process of restoration that went far beyond the nationalistic aspirations of the Jews. It would bring about the restoration of all things – the fulfilment of every prophecy, including that of the new covenant, and the reconciliation of the entire cosmos (Acts 3:21; Col. 1:19–22).

Leader's Notes

Week 1: Inspiration

Read the Introduction to your group to enable folk
to understand who Jeremiah was and why he and his
message are so important for us today. This first session
focuses on Jeremiah's call and stresses that the call to
trust in the Lord incorporates the call to serve the Lord,
in particular by taking up the responsibility to proclaim
God's truth to the world.

The Opening Icebreaker provides an opportunity for
people to share the beginnings of their spiritual journeys
with one another. Try to keep these brief and to the
point. One way is to use a three-minute egg timer! Ask
different people then to read the Bible passages and
particularly note the key verse. Ensure that you do this
each week.

Many Christians still believe quite wrongly that
proclaiming God's Word is a task for the specialist, the
trained leader or exceptionally gifted. Yet we share a
corporate calling as members of the Body of Christ and
all of us have a part to play in this, even if we are not
preachers or teachers. This may make some members
of the group uneasy and this is a good opportunity to
remind them that Jeremiah felt uneasy also. In fact he
complained that he was both too young and had nothing
to say. God reminded Jeremiah that he was chosen before
birth. This will be the place to look again at Psalm 139
and to encourage people to see just how secure they are
in the purposes of God for their lives. We are individually
known and loved by Him before we are born and the
way we have turned out is due to His weaving of us in
our mother's womb.

Jeremiah's mission was confrontational; he was to destroy unrighteous strongholds and then to plant justice in the land. In an age of bland political correctness we must not be afraid to tell the truth because it is the truth that liberates people from injustice and guilt. Remind people that the gospel has always been a challenge to deceit and hypocrisy but it is also God's way of salvation. As with Jeremiah we may just have to be unpopular because we tell the truth.

Use the Discussion Starters to raise people's awareness of what it means to be messengers of the kingdom of God in an age of unbelief, cynicism and unrighteousness. When focusing their attention on the sins of the nation ensure that this is done across the political spectrum and is not just a matter of selective morality, eg complaining about abortion but not about urban poverty or homelessness. Encourage a fresh awareness of God's willingness to speak to us by His Spirit in dreams and visions.

Use the Personal Application to encourage a prophetic spirit among your group members so that they will have the courage to speak out to their generation. Prophecy is more than foretelling the future; it is telling forth the truth, whether by proclamatory preaching or by exercising the gift of prophecy to hit the mark with the shaft of God's Word. Remind them that Jesus fearlessly challenged the status quo and that He did so in order to set people free. It will be good for the group to pray together for a sense of destiny about their lives and for the courage and compassion to proclaim God's truth to their circle of influence and beyond.

Week 2: Proclamation

Proclamation is about declaring truth and the Opening Icebreaker serves to remind us that our neighbours probably know very little about the gospel or about what God requires of those made in His image.

Spiritual adultery is a powerful metaphor that is repeatedly used by the prophets to describe idolatry. In most cases it does not consist of an outright rejection of God but begins with compromise and granting credence to other sources of spirituality in our lives – the equivalent of commencing an affair while still married. Disaster is seldom far away.

God sought to win Judah back, to warn her of her ways but in the end she was determined to follow the course of the idolatrous nations around her. In doing so she forfeited the blessings of the Creator in favour of worthless trash that, for all its pretensions, could not do anything to help.

Idolatry exacts a high price and leads to injustice, suffering and death. The fertility gods that Judah chose to follow required not only sexual promiscuity but also child abuse and child sacrifice. They also involved Judah's leaders in political deceit and treachery that filtered down until dishonesty and corruption had become a way of life throughout the nation.

Help your group to be aware of the subtle pressures to accept all religions as valid. We need to distinguish between the right of people to practise their religion, along with their entitlement to respect as human beings, from a requirement that we must somehow agree with their faith and accept it as being just as true as our own. That really does not have to follow.

Use the Discussion Starters to explore the dangers of spiritual adultery in the Church. Draw out the fact that the Church is called to be a prophetic voice in society but it can only do that as it remains uncompromised in belief and keeps its own house in order.

It is considered superstitious to see a connection between sin and disaster, but is this the case? Has God changed, or have we replaced Him with blind evolutionary chance? The Scriptures suggest that at the national level if not the personal there is a connection.

Since idolatry produces injustice, try to identify the vulnerable in our society and suggest ways to help them. This may mean we need to speak out prophetically and to challenge the indifference of our consumerist society to the price we exact from others to maintain our lifestyle.

You don't have to be a rabid fundamentalist to believe that others are wrong. The right to practise our faith must include the right to state that we disagree with those of other faiths. That is different from outright personal attacks on someone of another belief system. Explore how we find this balance in a society that increasingly restricts freedom of speech.

Use the Personal Application and Seeing Jesus sections to challenge one another to be true to our Creator and to the uniqueness of our Saviour. Idolatry takes many subtle forms and often comes down to the gradual supplanting of 'God territory' by other resources. The kingdom of God means that He comes first in all aspects of our thought, devotion and conduct and that we look to Him alone to meet our every need.

Week 3: Supplication

Everyone prays at some time in their lives, usually when they are in trouble or concerned about the wellbeing of their nearest and dearest. Use the Opening Icebreaker to invite members of your group to talk about the occasions that provoked their most profound prayers. You might like to find out if those prayers were answered.

There is a marked contrast between the prayer life of churches and individuals in nations that are experiencing spiritual awakening and nations, such as Great Britain, that are in the spiritual doldrums. Even a cursory question will soon evince the sheepish response that we don't pray as we ought and when we do our prayers are largely concerned with our personal and immediate needs.

We need to open our eyes to the spiritually needy state of our nation and the social implications of our ongoing rejection of Jesus. Most of us have plenty of material comfort but people are distressed. Even children are now on tranquillisers; almost half do not have the benefit of two parents at home. The fertility of the nation is at risk because of sexually contracted diseases that are now at epidemic proportions. Addictions are the major cause of premature death. Crime and the fear of crime is rife. Loss of respect, bad language, antisocial behaviour, make up the daily diet of our media. The list can go on. It would be good if you found a creative way of presenting some of this to your group, perhaps using news clips or newspaper cuttings to make the point.

Our job is to pray. Indeed, Paul laid it as a solemn responsibility upon Timothy. Yet our prayers must not be dispassionate. We need to capture again a sense of earnestness, of weeping and anguish over the condition of society. Nor can we detach ourselves from it in self-righteous arrogance. We may be citizens of heaven and pilgrims on earth, but while we live here we are part of society and need to identify with the sinfulness of the nation. Isaiah considered himself to dwell among a people of unclean lips but he acknowledged the uncleanness of his own lips also.

So bad was the situation that Jeremiah had little chance of his prayers being answered, but that was not the point. Every person who prays for repentance pleases God and keeps open the doors of possibility. Who knows what might change because we pray?

When you come to Discussion Starter 3 you might like between you to write such a prayer and to formally pray it together.

Because unanswered prayer makes us desperate we may find ourselves questioning God. Discussion Starter 4 reflects on when Jeremiah did this, accusing God of becoming 'a deceitful brook and waters that fail.' Use this incident to help us not make the same mistake.

Organising a prayer walk is simple. You choose the time and the roads and just walk around in twos or threes praying for whatever your eyes see and the Spirit of God lays upon you. You'll be surprised how effective it is.

The probable answer to Discussion Starter 7 is that, as far as Britain is concerned, we are in the balance. It makes supplication all the more urgent a need.

Encourage folk to build prayer for the nation into their daily devotions and try to ensure that it happens during your corporate gatherings. Remind everyone that their intercessions are an identification with Christ's ongoing passion for the world to be saved.

Week 4: Confrontation

Truth telling is fast becoming a lost art in a society that has lost its moral and spiritual foundations. Many of the problems we face today, whether at a personal or national level, are the result of either an unwillingness to confront the real issues or because of deliberate deceit to cover up error and corruption. Spin doctors do not sit comfortably with Jesus' words: 'Simply let your "Yes" be "Yes", and your "No", "No"; anything beyond this comes from the evil one' (Matt. 5:37).

Use the Opening Icebreaker to draw out incidents when folk have had the courage to confront others with the truth. These may be in family or business matters.

It used to be said that politics and religion don't mix, but of course they do because both have to do with society and its conduct and beliefs. However, the politics of the kingdom of God is not about the policies embraced by particular political parties but rather is concerned with moral and spiritual truth. Jeremiah unavoidably discovered that faithfulness to God meant speaking out politically on issues of righteousness and justice.

To judge by the reaction he provoked he obviously hit the mark. Like Jesus he became a threat to the establishment and it was simply a matter of time before his own life was under threat. In this, Jeremiah showed great courage and determination even though he found the pain of confrontation very real and frightening.

God had promised that He would address government and Jeremiah finds himself at odds with the court officials, the king and the soothsayers, all of whom prophesy peace. Yet, Jeremiah, his sound political judgment informed by the Word of God, is obliged to disagree and to stand alone, ridiculed and hated.

Challenging the vested interests of those in political and religious power is never easy, yet we must be prepared to do it. The majority really can be wrong! Use the Discussion Starters to explore how we can engage in 'the controversy of truth' in a decadent age. This needs to be faced personally by each one of us since we all face situations where we must make a stand. Remind folk that we should be gracious in how we do it, but that however nice we are truth will always sting those who oppose it.

We also need to face the truth in our churches and not simply cover up areas where we need to change our ways. This is not an invitation to self-destructive criticism so much as a call for corporate humility, particularly in respect of our claims to be loving, outreaching and empowered witnesses to Christ's message.

Jeremiah's courage should be an inspiration to us and should motivate us to speak up on behalf of the oppressed. It also challenges us not simply to talk about love but to make it practical. Sometimes, for example, parents will talk about loving their children but will never correct them when they are straying, or will not share the gospel with them. That is a false love. Jesus loved us enough to tell the truth. He calls us to do the same.

Encourage the group to pray for one another over issues where members need the moral fibre to tell the truth. Agree that you will support one another in this and will seek God together for wisdom whenever this is deemed appropriate.

Week 5: Devastation

The world ends for all of us at some time or other, if only when we die, but it will end as we know it at the return of Christ. With people everywhere recognising a time limit on this planet's existence, use the Opening Icebreaker to examine the various ideas around at present and focus your group on the certain promise of Christ's return.

This session is about another end of the world, a time when all the security of centuries is destroyed by war. Try to imagine the blindness of the people of Jerusalem as they lived in their fool's paradise, blithely ignoring that mad prophet, Jeremiah. Imagine the anger of the rulers when they heard his words advocating surrender to the enemy because the only way to receive mercy was to submit to the judgment of God for their sins.

Then the horror begins, invasion, siege, famine, chaos within a city destroying itself, and finally the breach of the walls and the invading army flooding in, killing indiscriminately, looting and putting the city to the flames. A whole history and culture consumed in days.

Consider the plight of the survivors, the best of them chained together with hooks though their noses and stripped bare for a forced march of over 500 miles to Babylon, raped, abused and dying by the score as they struggled across the wilderness.

How does Jeremiah feel? His message proved to be the truth and Nebuchadnezzar set him free in acknowledge-ment of that fact, no doubt thinking that the prophet was on his side. Yet it gave Jeremiah no pleasure to see judgment fall, especially because had they heeded his words it would have been averted. Nor are his own troubles over. A bunch of superstitious refugees insist that he accompany them on a futile journey to Egypt and this man of God once again has to warn of the folly of worshipping the very idols that had caused the trouble in the first place.

Use the Discussion Starters to talk about disasters and their effects on us. God by preference likes to show mercy but there are times when divine patience is exhausted and He shows judgment. War is one such expression of judgment. We, by our prayers and devotion to Him, play a key role in preserving peace in our world.

Disasters invite reflection. How do we still believe in a God of love? Perhaps that is unanswerable in this life, but we can use our anger, frustration and pain as a springboard to action. We can make a difference, offering mercy and succour to the victims – and we can keep the faith in spite of the faithlessness around us. Even when God judges, He is still our Rock and Fortress and Deliverer. We have this comfort to offer to all who will listen.

This world will end in judgment at the return of Christ. Horrific as this may seem it is a cause for celebration because the evils that have dogged the human race, the injustices of the world, will finally be dealt with. This judgment will be a cleansing, as ultimately was the case with Jerusalem, and it will usher in a renewed cosmos where evil is for ever banished. Help your group understand the bracing nature of the judgment scenario and remind them of Peter's injunction: 'Since everything will be destroyed in this way, what kind of people ought you to be? You ought to live holy and godly lives as you look forward to the day of God and speed its coming' (2 Pet. 3:11–12).

Week 6: Lamentation

This session may prove to be one of the most honest you
have ever had as we strip the veneer from dealing with
grief by avoidance and by offering superficial platitudes.
The Opening Icebreaker invites people to talk about
sadness. Do not worry if this is an emotional time. It's
meant to be!

Jeremiah was fated to look upon the destruction of
everything he and his people had held dear. He saw
horrors that were beyond comprehension as his city was
torn to pieces and his people, already starving to death,
were raped, tortured and slaughtered by a zealous and
implacable foe. Worse, Jeremiah was all too mindful that
it had come about because the nation had forsaken God
and given itself over to idolatry. This was judgment day.

How does Jeremiah respond to all this horror? He
could have said as a true prophet, 'I told you so.' He
might, as one of the righteous elect, have detached
himself from involvement and have offered a theological
and sociological analysis. Having been freed by
Nebuchadnezzar he might have fled from the scene with
a sense of relief. Instead, he embraces the grief of the
situation and gives voice to it in a series of laments that
constitute the book of that name.

We are a death-denying society often inured to the
sufferings of the world because of image saturation by
our media. Only when it comes close do we respond,
but then often superficially. Too often it is left to the
secular poets to voice the anger and anguish, but they
can be cynical. Surely we who follow the Man of Sorrows
should know how to lament the horrors of this world.
Bereavement in all its forms is not to be denied and
repressed but faced with integrity. Take the opportunity

to do so in your group meeting. You might wish to pick up on some of those sad stories or to consider some of the grievous situations around you. You may wish to attempt writing a lament between you and reading it out.

Use the Discussion Starters to open up the various dimensions to this important theme. Some in your group may be facile triumphalists who will not like this 'gloomy' emphasis. Remind them that the power of lament lies in its ability to cleanse us and prepare us for the future. Jeremiah's lament acknowledged the sins of the people and came to terms with the consequences. It also contains the seeds of hope that God is still good and His mercies are daily renewed even during times of trouble.

Some in your group will want to face their griefs honestly and you should provide a supportive context of prayer and personal ministry where appropriate. Bereavement takes many forms, from the loss of a loved one to the loss of a career, a bodily impairment, a lost opportunity, broken families, failed exams and so forth. It is proper to grieve and to express that in lament. Encourage everyone to read through the whole book of Lamentations and instead of just looking for the bright verses like nuggets in the mud to recognise that the whole is liquid gold. By entering the feelings of grief we come to appreciate hope all the more. Finally, remind your group that Jesus understood grief and did not duck from its emotions. He understands the human condition and is there to sustain us in its worse moments as well as its best.

Week 7: Restoration

This final session turns the tragedy of Jeremiah's ministry into a comedy of grace. God's plan is not destruction but purification and restoration. The captivity was ruinous but it finally purged God's people from their obsession with fertility cult worship. Use the Opening Icebreaker to talk about what is involved in the process of restoration based upon people's own experiences.

The captivity in Babylon was where the future lay. Jeremiah's vision of the two baskets of figs indicates that what remained in Jerusalem was corrupted but what survived in Babylon carried the seeds of hope for the future. The captivity was destined to last 70 years to pay off the debt owed to the land for all the broken Sabbaths – an interesting principle that you might like to explore in our contemporary world without rest.

Analysing the scene, Jeremiah discerned that the people had been led astray by false shepherds. God will send His true Shepherd, the Messiah, Jesus, who will lay down His life for the sheep. At that time the Lord will make a new covenant with His people. Try not to get into the debate about modern-day Israel and the extent to which this is a nationalistic promise for the future. Instead, concentrate on what is clear: this new covenant promise is the gospel that Jesus and the apostles preached. All Jews who receive Jesus as their Messiah enter into it, and all Gentiles who do the same are grafted into that same covenant. Spend some time focusing on the blessings that are promised – the gift of the Holy Spirit, heart obedience to God's will, belonging to God's holy nation, personal relationship with the Lord, the forgiveness of sins.

You may like to use the restoration promise as a metaphor for the spiritual transformation that occurs when we, alienated people, are brought back into fellowship with God through the cross of Christ. Emphasise the spiritual principle that life springs from death and that we should affirm life and hope and goodness. Without being superficial (for we pass through our 'dying to self'; we don't bypass it) we should rejoice constantly in our new-found life in Christ.

Use the Discussion Starters to explore this great principle of death leading to life. It is central to Jesus' teaching and to His passion. Accepting the spiral of dying and rising that constitutes our spiritual experience, and seeing that the Spirit of God is at work to bring us to Christlikeness through the process, helps us to make sense of life and gain the growth benefit from each season. You may wish to pick up on the story of the Prodigal Son to help any who are away from the Lord at the present time to find the courage to return. As with Jeremiah, we will discover that God is ultimately our loving Father, not our executioner judge.

Restoration is the ultimate goal of God's plan in Christ. The day will come when all things are put to rights, all evil dealt with, and life will triumph over death for ever. Encourage your group to invest in that future by their prayers, good works, celebration and thanksgiving, just as Jeremiah invested in his field in anticipation of the return of God's people to their land. You may like to end this series with a celebratory act that captures something of the joy and amazement of God's captive people when at length they were set free and allowed to return to their homeland.

NATIONAL DISTRIBUTORS

UK: (and countries not listed below)
CWR, Waverley Abbey House, Waverley Lane, Farnham, Surrey GU9 8EP.
Tel: (01252) 784700 Outside UK (44) 1252 784700 Email: mail@cwr.org.uk

AUSTRALIA: KI Entertainment, Unit 21 317-321 Woodpark Road, Smithfield,
New South Wales 2164.
Tel: 1 800 850 777 Fax: 02 9604 3699 Email: sales@kientertainment.com.au

CANADA: David C Cook Distribution Canada, PO Box 98, 55 Woodslee Avenue,
Paris, Ontario N3L 3E5.
Tel: 1800 263 2664 Email: swansons@cook.ca

GHANA: Challenge Enterprises of Ghana, PO Box 5723, Accra.
Tel: (021) 222437/223249 Fax: (021) 226227 Email: ceg@africaonline.com.gh

HONG KONG: Cross Communications Ltd, 1/F, 562A Nathan Road, Kowloon.
Tel: 2780 1188 Fax: 2770 6229 Email: cross@crosshk.com

INDIA: Crystal Communications, 10-3-18/4/1, East Marredpalli, Secunderabad
– 500026, Andhra Pradesh.
Tel/Fax: (040) 27737145 Email: crystal_edwj@rediffmail.com

KENYA: Keswick Books and Gifts Ltd, PO Box 10242-00400, Nairobi.
Tel: (254) 20 312639/3870125 Email: keswick@swiftkenya.com

MALAYSIA: Salvation Book Centre (M) Sdn Bhd, 23 Jalan SS 2/64,
47300 Petaling Jaya, Selangor.
Tel: (03) 78766411/78766797 Fax: (03) 78757066/78756360
Email: info@salvationbookcentre.com

Canaanland, No. 25 Jalan PJU 1A/41B, NZX Commercial Centre, Ara Jaya,
47301 Petaling Jaya, Selangor.
Tel: (03) 7885 0540/1/2 Fax: (03) 7885 0545 Email: info@canaanland.com.my

NEW ZEALAND: KI Entertainment, Unit 21 317-321 Woodpark Road, Smithfield,
New South Wales 2164, Australia.
Tel: 0 800 850 777 Fax: +612 9604 3699 Email: sales@kientertainment.com.au

NIGERIA: FBFM, Helen Baugh House, 96 St Finbarr's College Road, Akoka, Lagos.
Tel: (01) 7747429/4700218/825775/827264 Email: fbfm@hyperia.com

PHILIPPINES: OMF Literature Inc, 776 Boni Avenue, Mandaluyong City.
Tel: (02) 531 2183 Fax: (02) 531 1960 Email: gloadlaon@omflit.com

SINGAPORE: Alby Commercial Enterprises Pte Ltd, 95 Kallang Avenue #04-00,
AIS Industrial Building, 339420.
Tel: (65) 629 27238 Fax: (65) 629 27235 Email: marketing@alby.com.sg

SOUTH AFRICA: Struik Christian Books, 80 MacKenzie Street, PO Box 1144,
Cape Town 8000.
Tel: (021) 462 4360 Fax: (021) 461 3612 Email: info@struikchristianmedia.co.za

SRI LANKA: Christombu Publications (Pvt) Ltd, Bartleet House, 65 Braybrooke
Place, Colombo 2.
Tel: (9411) 2421073/2447665 Email: dhanad@bartleet.com

USA: David C Cook Distribution Canada, PO Box 98, 55 Woodslee Avenue, Paris,
Ontario N3L 3E5, Canada. Tel: 1800 263 2664 Email: swansons@cook.ca

CWR is a Registered Charity - Number 294387
CWR is a Limited Company registered in England -
Registration Number 1990308

Day and Residential Courses
Counselling Training
Leadership Development
Biblical Study Courses
Regional Seminars
Ministry to Women
Daily Devotionals
Books and DVDs
Conference Centre

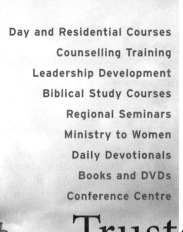

Trusted all Over the World

CWR HAS GAINED A WORLDWIDE reputation as a centre of excellence for Bible-based training and resources. From our headquarters at Waverley Abbey House, Farnham, England, we have been serving God's people for over 40 years with a vision to help apply God's Word to everyday life and relationships. The daily devotional *Every Day with Jesus* is read by nearly a million people in more than 150 countries, and our unique courses in biblical studies and pastoral care are respected all over the world. Waverley Abbey House provides a conference centre in a tranquil setting.

For free brochures on our seminars and courses, conference facilities, or a catalogue of CWR resources, please contact us at the following address.
CWR, Waverley Abbey House, Waverley Lane, Farnham, Surrey GU9 8EP, UK

Telephone: **+44 (0)1252 784700**
Email: **mail@cwr.org.uk**
Website: **www.cwr.org.uk**

Applying God's Word
to everyday life and relationships

Dramatic new resources

2 Corinthians: Restoring harmony
by Christine Platt

Paul's message went against the grain of the culture in Corinth, and even his humility was in stark contrast to Greco–Roman culture. Be challenged and inspired to endure suffering, seek reconciliation, pursue holiness and much more as you look at this moving letter which reveals Paul's heart as much as his doctrine. This thought-provoking, seven-week study guide is great for individual or small-group use.
ISBN: 978-1-85345-551-3

Isaiah 40–66: Prophet of restoration
by John Houghton

God is a God of new beginnings, a God of second chances who takes no pleasure in punishment. However, profound lessons must be learned if the same errors are to be avoided in the future. Understand Isaiah's powerful message for each of us, that God is a holy God who cannot ignore sin, but One who also displays amazing grace and mercy, and who longs to enjoy restored relationship with us. These seven inspiring and challenging studies are perfect for individual or small-group use.
ISBN: 978-1-85345-550-6

Also available in the bestselling
Cover to Cover Bible Study Series

1 Corinthians
Growing a Spirit-filled church
ISBN: 978-1-85345-374-8

Esther
For such a time as this
ISBN: 978-1-85345-511-7

2 Corinthians
Restoring harmony
ISBN: 978-1-85345-551-3

Fruit of the Spirit
Growing more like Jesus
ISBN: 978-1-85345-375-5

1 Timothy
Healthy churches – effective Christians
ISBN: 978-1-85345-291-8

Genesis 1–11
Foundations of reality
ISBN: 978-1-85345-404-2

23rd Psalm
The Lord is my shepherd
ISBN: 978-1-85345-449-3

God's Rescue Plan
Finding God's fingerprints on human history
ISBN: 978-1-85345-294-9

2 Timothy and Titus
Vital Christianity
ISBN: 978-1-85345-338-0

Great Prayers of the Bible
Applying them to our lives today
ISBN: 978-1-85345-253-6

Ecclesiastes
Hard questions and spiritual answers
ISBN: 978-1-85345-371-7

Hebrews
Jesus – simply the best
ISBN: 978-1-85345-337-3

Ephesians
Claiming your inheritance
ISBN: 978-1-85345-229-1

Hosea
The love that never fails
ISBN: 978-1-85345-290-1

£3.99 each (plus p&p)

Price correct at time of printing

Cover to Cover Every Day
Gain deeper knowledge of the Bible

Each issue of these bimonthly daily Bible-reading notes gives you insightful commentary on a book of the Old and New Testaments with reflections on a Psalm each weekend by Philip Greenslade.

Enjoy contributions from two well-known authors every two months, and over a five-year period you will be taken through the entire Bible.

ISSN: 1744-0114
Only £2.49 each (plus p&p)
£13.80 for annual UK subscription (6 issues)
£13.80 for annual email subscription
(available from www.cwr.org.uk/store)

Cover to Cover Complete
Read through the Bible chronologically

Take an exciting, year-long journey through the Bible, following events as they happened.

- See God's strategic plan of redemption unfold across the centuries
- Increase your confidence in the Bible as God's inspired message
- Come to know your heavenly Father in a deeper way

The full text of the flowing Holman Christian Standard Bible (HCSB) provides an exhilarating reading experience and is augmented by our beautiful:

- Illustrations
- Maps
- Charts
- Diagrams
- Timeline

And key Scripture verses and devotional thoughts make each day's reading more meaningful.

ISBN: 978-1-85345-433-2
Only £19.99 (plus p&p)

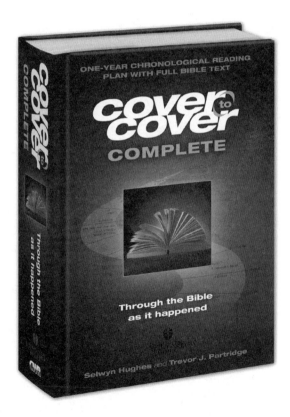